DESCUBRAMOS
PAÍSES DEL MUNDO

Descubramos países del
CARIBE

Jillian Powell

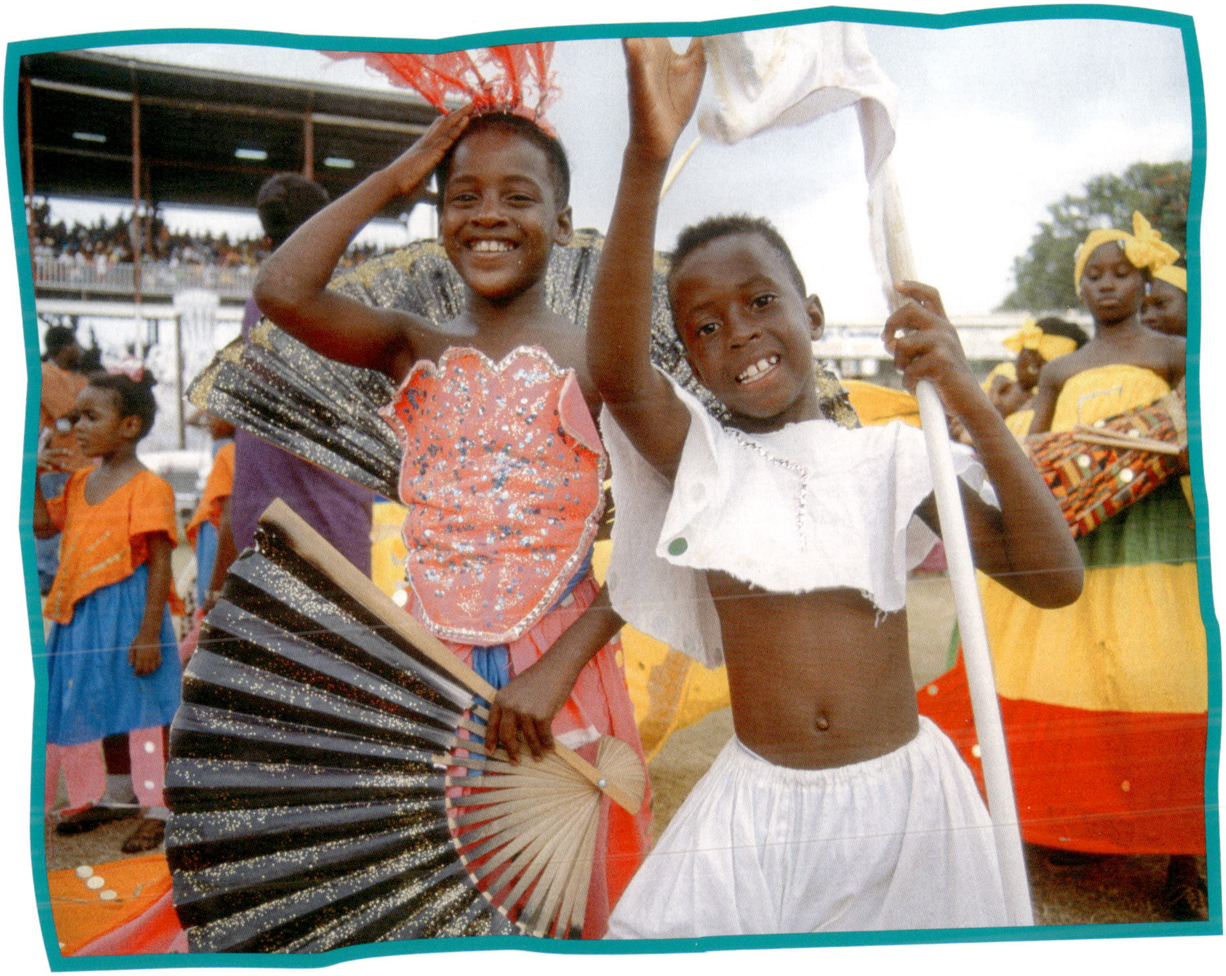

Please visit our web site at: www.garethstevens.com
For a free color catalog describing Gareth Stevens Publishing's list
of high-quality books and multimedia programs, call 1-800-542-2595 (USA)
or 1-800-387-3178 (Canada). Gareth Stevens Publishing's fax: (414) 332-3567.

Library of Congress Cataloging-in-Publication Data available upon request from publisher.
Fax (414) 336-0157 for the attention of the Publishing Records Department.

ISBN-13: 978-0-8368-7957-5 (lib.bdg.)
ISBN-13: 978-0-8368-7964-3 (softcover)

This North American edition first published in 2007 by
Gareth Stevens Publishing
A Member of the WRC Media Family of Companies
330 West Olive Street, Suite 100
Milwaukee, Wisconsin 53212 USA

This U.S. edition copyright © 2007 by Gareth Stevens, Inc.
Original edition copyright © 2006 by Franklin Watts.
First published in Great Britain in 2006 by Franklin Watts,
338 Euston Road, London NW1 3BH, United Kingdom.

Series editor: Sarah Peutrill
Art director: Jonathan Hair
Design: Rita Storey
Picture research: Diana Morris

Gareth Stevens editor: Dorothy L. Gibbs
Gareth Stevens art direction: Tammy West
Gareth Stevens graphic designer: Charlie Dahl

Spanish edition produced by A+ Media, Inc.
Editorial director: Julio Abreu
Chief translator: Adriana Rosado-Bonewitz
Associate editors: Janina Morgan, Carolyn Schildgen
Graphic design: Faith Weeks

Photo credits: (t=top, b=bottom, l=left, r=right, c=center)
Tony Arruza/Corbis: 25b. Yann Arthus-Bertrand/Corbis: 4. Tom Bean/Corbis: 8. Richard Bickel/Corbis: 17.
Jonathan Blair/Corbis: 7. Pablo Corral V/Corbis: 25t. Howard Davies/Corbis: 16. Eye Ubiquitous/Hutchison: 18, 23.
Kevin Fletcher/Corbis: 13. Owen Franken/Corbis: 15. Stephen Frink/Corbis: 20. Philippe Giraud/Sygma/Corbis: 19t.
R. Hackenburg/zefa/Corbis: 26. Glen Hinkson/Reuters/Corbis: 9b. Jeremy Horner/Panos Pictures: 27. Dave G. Houser/
Post-Houserstock/Corbis: 19b. Jonathan Kaplan/Still Pictures: 10. Bob Krist/Corbis: 11, 14. Buddy Mays/Corbis: 22.
Gideon Mendel/Corbis: 12. Helene Rogers/Alamy: 21c. Galen Rowell/Corbis: 6. Superbild/A1 Pix: cover, 1, 9t, 21t, 24.

Every effort has been made to trace the copyright holders for the photos used in this book. The publisher apologizes, in advance, for any unintentional omissions and would be pleased to insert the appropriate acknowledgements in any subsequent edition of this publication.

All rights reserved. No part of this book may be reproduced, stored in a retrieval system, or transmitted in any form or by any means, electronic, mechanical, photocopying, recording, or otherwise, without the prior written permission of the copyright holder.

Printed in Canada

1 2 3 4 5 6 7 8 9 10 10 09 08 07 06

Contenido

¿Dónde está el Caribe?	4
El paisaje	6
Clima y estaciones	8
La gente del Caribe	10
Escuela y familia	12
Vida rural	14
Vida urbana	16
Casas del Caribe	18
Comida del Caribe	20
El trabajo	22
La diversión	24
Países del Caribe: datos	26
Glosario	28
Para más información	29
Mi mapa del Caribe	30
Índice	32

Las palabras definidas en el glosario están impresas en **negritas** la primera vez que aparecen en el texto.

¿Dónde está el Caribe?

El Caribe es una región o área de los **trópicos** que se encuentra entre el Océano Atlántico y el Mar Caribe.

La región conocida como "el Caribe" se llama así por el Mar Caribe.

Incluye más de siete mil islas, así como también países que están en tierra firme como Belice, Guyana y Surinam.

Las islas del Caribe van desde Cuba, que es la más grande de las Antillas Mayores, hasta las más pequeñas como Bahamas y las Antillas Menores.

Esta vista desde el aire muestra varias islas pequeñas de las Antillas Menores.

El paisaje

El Caribe es famoso por sus hermosos paisajes que van de las montañas a las playas. Las montañas de muchas de las islas más grandes tienen altas cascadas y están cubiertas de selvas.

La isla de Santa Lucía tiene muchas montañas altas.

Barbados es una isla plana de colinas bajas.

Algunas de las islas más pequeñas, como Barbados y Antigua, tienen paisajes bajos y planos. Otras islas tienen **saladares** o áreas pantanosas donde crecen los **mangles**.

Las islas del Caribe están rodeadas por cálidos mares tropicales. Muchas tienen bahías con **arrecifes coralinos** y playas de arenas blancas.

¿Lo sabías?

La arena de las playas de Harbour Island, en Bahamas, es rosa.

Clima y estaciones

El Caribe tiene un clima tropical, lo que significa que hay mucho sol y llueve mucho. El tiempo es cálido todo el año con vientos frescos que soplan del Océano Atlántico.

Durante la temporada seca, que va de diciembre a mayo, el tiempo es muy cálido con pocas lluvias.

La selva tropical en la isla de Puerto Rico se llama El Yunque. Es el Bosque Nacional del Caribe.

El clima cálido y las bellas playas atraen a los turistas a la República Dominicana y a otras islas del Caribe.

La temporada húmeda, que va de junio a noviembre, tiene fuertes lluvias e inundaciones. Entre julio y octubre las tormentas se convierten a veces en huracanes. Los vientos de los huracanes soplan a velocidades de hasta 300 kilómetros (185 millas) por hora.

¿Lo sabías?

Cada año, se llama a los huracanes con nombres propios que inician con las letras del abecedario.

Los huracanes destruyen edificios y cultivos y pueden acabar con ciudades enteras. En Granada, un huracán causó estos daños.

La gente del Caribe

Los caribeños provienen de razas y **culturas** diferentes, especialmente de Europa, África y Asia. Muy pocos tienen **antepasados** arahuacos o caribes. Los arahuacos y los caribes son los **amerindios** que poblaron originalmente la región del Caribe.

Algunos de los idiomas que se hablan en los países caribeños son español, inglés, holandés y francés. Algunos caribeños hablan **patúa** o **criollo**. Estos idiomas locales son una mezcla de inglés e idiomas europeos o africanos.

Este guyanés trabaja como leñador. Sus antepasados eran amerindios.

Estas personas de las Islas Vírgenes Británicas salen de un servicio religioso cristiano.

Muchos caribeños son cristianos, algunos son musulmanes, hindúes, o **rastafaris** y algunos practican religiones africanas que adoran a sus propios dioses o antepasados.

¿Lo sabías?

La religión rastafari comenzó en Jamaica, que es la tercera isla más grande del Caribe.

Escuela y familia

La mayoría de los niños caribeños va a la escuela desde los cinco años. Van a la secundaria, o preparatoria, más o menos entre los 11 y los 15 años. Después, algunos siguen en la escuela y otros aprenden oficios o comienzan a trabajar.

Estas niñas de Haití van a una escuela de una plantación en la República Dominicana porque sus padres trabajan ahí.

Estos niños juegan béisbol en una calle poco transitada de Trinidad.

Muchas familias caribeñas no tienen mucho dinero y los niños pobres no tienen suficiente ropa o juguetes. A menudo inventan sus propios juegos, usando bates y pelotas y otros juguetes que ellos mismos hacen.

Los niños más pobres de Haití son los de la calle. Algunos son **huérfanos** y no tienen casa, educación o servicios de salud. Los programas de caridad tratan de hacerse cargo de estos niños.

Vida rural

En las Bahamas, las mujeres a menudo llevan su mercancía sobre la cabeza cuando van a los mercados.

La gente que vive en las áreas rurales a veces tiene tierras en las que cultivan verduras o crían animales como cabras.

Algunas veces las mujeres llevan sus productos a los mercados y los venden para ganar dinero. A lo largo de los caminos rurales hay puestos donde venden frutas y verduras.

En las playas caribeñas, la gente vende pescado fresco.

En esta plantación de la Martinica, la caña de azúcar se cosecha con maquinaria.

La población rural caribeña también trabaja en las plantaciones de caña de azúcar, en los platanales o en los cafetales. Aunque la maquinaria agrícola se usa en muchas plantaciones, todavía se cosecha a mano.

¿Lo sabías?

Las frutas y verduras cultivadas en las plantaciones caribeñas se venden en todo el mundo.

Vida urbana

Aproximadamente tres cuartas partes de la población caribeña vive en ciudades. Los lugares más poblados son las capitales, incluyendo Kingston, en Jamaica, La Habana, en Cuba y Puerto Príncipe, en Haití.

El distrito comercial de Kingston, la capital de Jamaica, tiene muchos edificios de oficinas.

Las capitales de los países caribeños han crecido rápidamente. Estas ciudades tienen muchos edificios de varios pisos con bancos, oficinas, tiendas y museos.

Para transportarse en Puerto Príncipe, mucha gente sube a autobuses de colores brillantes como éste.

¿Lo sabías?

La Habana tiene "camellos" que llevan a cientos de personas. Estos autobuses tienen forma de joroba de camello.

Las calles caribeñas están llenas de autobuses, camiones, taxis y bicicletas. Los autobuses tap-tap de Haití y los coco taxis de La Habana son de brillantes colores.

Casas del Caribe

Existen muchos estilos diferentes de casas en los países caribeños.

En los **suburbios**, mucha gente vive en edificios de apartamentos. La más rica vive en casas propias. Sus casas a menudo tienen jardines y características modernas como televisión satelital y aire acondicionado.

Estas niñas caminan de la escuela a sus casas en La Habana, Cuba. Viven en grandes edificios de apartamentos en la ciudad.

Los más pobres de las ciudades caribeñas viven en las afueras o zonas suburbanas, en amontonadas viviendas hechas de pedazos de metal, cartón y madera, sin electricidad ni agua corriente.

Una casa caribeña típica está hecha de madera y pintada de brillantes colores.

En las áreas rurales caribeñas, muchas casas son **búngalos** de madera de una sola planta con techos de lámina o **palma**. Muchas tienen porches cubiertos o **terrazas** y la mayoría tiene persianas que pueden cerrarse para mantener la casa fresca.

Estas casas de madera de Barbados se desarman y se vuelven a construir cuando las familias se mudan para encontrar trabajo.

¿Lo sabías?

El poblado de Mandeville, en Jamaica, tiene cabañas estilo inglés alrededor de un jardín comunitario.

Comida del Caribe

La comida caribeña combina muchas cocinas, incluyendo la europea, la africana y la asiática, además de la arahuaca y la del Caribe. El puerco en salsa "jerk" es un conocido plato arahuaco de Jamaica de carne a la barbacoa. Las especias son muy importantes en la cocina caribeña. Muchos platos combinan frutas con carne o pescado salado.

La "comida rápida" en el Caribe significa a menudo comida cocinada al momento en un puesto, como éste en Puerto Rico.

Este mercado de plátanos al aire libre en San Martín está justo en la playa.

Este supermercado de Santa Lucía ofrece una gran variedad de frutas y verduras.

Otros platos caribeños incluyen arroz y chícharos en leche de coco y sopas o guisados con pescado salado y tubérculos. En los mercados al aire libre y en los supermercados se venden muchas frutas como mangos y plátanos, y tubérculos como la **yuca**, las papas y ñame (o boniato).

¿Lo sabías?

A Granada se le llama la "isla de las especias". ¡Hasta la nuez moscada aparece en la bandera del país!

La diversión

Los caribeños aman los festivales, la música y el baile. Durante el Carnaval, llevan disfraces coloridos y desfilan a pie o en carrozas por las calles de la ciudad.

¿Lo sabías?

En Antigua, hay carreras de cangrejos todas las semanas.

Para los niños, Carnaval significa "diversión".

Los instrumentos de una banda de percusión caribeña parecen enormes cacerolas de metal.

Las bandas, el **calipso** y el **reggae** son estilos musicales de los países caribeños. En Puerto Rico y Cuba, la gente baila en clubes, fiestas y hasta en las calles.

Los deportes también son actividades populares. A los caribeños les gusta ver los partidos de básquetbol, **críquet** y fútbol. Durante la temporada de calor, a los niños les encanta jugar afuera al tenis callejero o al críquet de playa.

Esta playa de Barbados es un buen lugar para el críquet de playa.

Países del Caribe: datos

- El Caribe está compuesto de 32 países. Quince de ellos son miembros de pleno derecho de la Comunidad del Caribe (CARICOM). La región del Caribe también incluye miembros de habla hispana como Cuba y República Dominicana, junto con territorios que pertenecen a Gran Bretaña, Francia, los Países Bajos y Estados Unidos.

- La región del Caribe tiene tres grupos principales de islas: las Bahamas, las Antillas Mayores y las Antillas Menores. Las islas más grandes están en las Antillas Mayores.

Cada país del Caribe tiene su propia bandera. Esta bandera es la de Cuba.

La Habana, Cuba, es la capital más grande de los países del Caribe, donde viven más de dos millones de personas.

- Las monedas principales o tipos de dinero que se usan en los países del Caribe incluyen el dólar del Caribe Oriental, el dólar de Estados Unidos y el euro. En Cuba y la República Dominicana, la moneda principal es el peso.

¿Lo sabías?

El Mar Caribe se llama así por los caribes, que fueron los primeros pobladores de las islas.

Glosario

amerindios – nativos originales de las Américas

antepasados – miembros de la familia que vivieron en el pasado

arrecifes coralinos – colinas de coral que se elevan del lecho marino

búngalos – casas pequeñas de una planta

calipso – música animada de las Antillas, acompañada de canciones sobre sucesos divertidos

criollo – mezcla de inglés y francés

críquet – conocido deporte británico en equipos que se juega con bates y pelotas y que no se parece al béisbol

culturas – las costumbres y creencias de ciertas civilizaciones, nacionalidades, sociedades u otros grupos humanos

desalinización – proceso para retirar la sal del agua marina

huérfanos – niños sin padres vivos

mangles – árboles tropicales que crecen en el agua salada en las costas y que tienen raíces que parecen zancos

palma – material vegetal como el pasto, la paja, o las ramas usadas como techo

patúa – dialecto del inglés que hablan los afro-jamaicanos

plantación – granjas grandes donde se cosechan café y plátanos para vender en los mercados locales y en el extranjero

rastafaris – gente que sigue el movimiento rastafari, una religión que surge de los afro-jamaicanos

reggae – estilo de música que mezcla los ritmos jamaicanos nativos con el rock y el soul

saladares – tierras húmedas bajas cerca del mar

suburbios – áreas que rodean una gran ciudad, donde vive la gente que trabaja en la ciudad

terrazas – porches cubiertos o áreas abiertas a lo largo del frente o los lados de las casas

trópicos – regiones cálidas y húmedas de la Tierra cercanas al ecuador

yuca – planta tropical cuya raíz contiene almidón que se usa para espesar alimentos líquidos

Para más información

Boricua Kids (History of Puerto Rico for Children)
www.elboricua.com/BoricuaKids.html

Caribbean National Forest Kids Page
www.fs.fed.us/r8/caribbean/kids-page/

Eye on the Caribbean
www.globaleye.org.uk/primary_autumn04/eyeon/intro.html

Talk Jamaican!
www.jamaicans.com/speakja/talk.htm

Nota del editor para educadores y padres: Nuestros editores han revisado cuidadosamente estos sitios Web para asegurarse de que son apropiados para niños. Sin embargo, muchos sitios Web cambian con frecuencia, y no podemos asegurar que el contenido futuro del sitio seguirá satisfaciendo nuestros estándares altos de calidad y valor educativo. Se le advierte que se debe supervisar estrechamente a los niños siempre que tengan acceso al Internet.

Mi mapa del Caribe

Fotocopia o calca el mapa de la página 31. Después, escribe los nombres de los grupos de islas, extensiones de agua, países y capitales que se listan a continuación. (Mira el mapa de la página 5 si necesitas ayuda.)

Después de escribir los nombres de todos los lugares, ¡colorea el mapa con crayones!

Grupos de islas
Antillas Mayores
Antillas Menores
Bahamas
Islas Vírgenes Británicas
Islas Vírgenes de los
   Estados Unidos

Extensiones de agua
Mar Caribe
Océano Atlántico

Países en tierra firme
Belice
Guyana
Surinam

Capitales
Kingston
La Habana
Puerto Príncipe
San Juan

Países insulares
Antigua y Barbuda
Barbados
Cuba
Dominica
Granada
Guadalupe
Haití
Jamaica
Martinica
Puerto Rico
República Dominicana
San Cristóbal y Nevis
San Martín
San Vicente y las Granadinas
Santa Lucía
Trinidad y Tobago

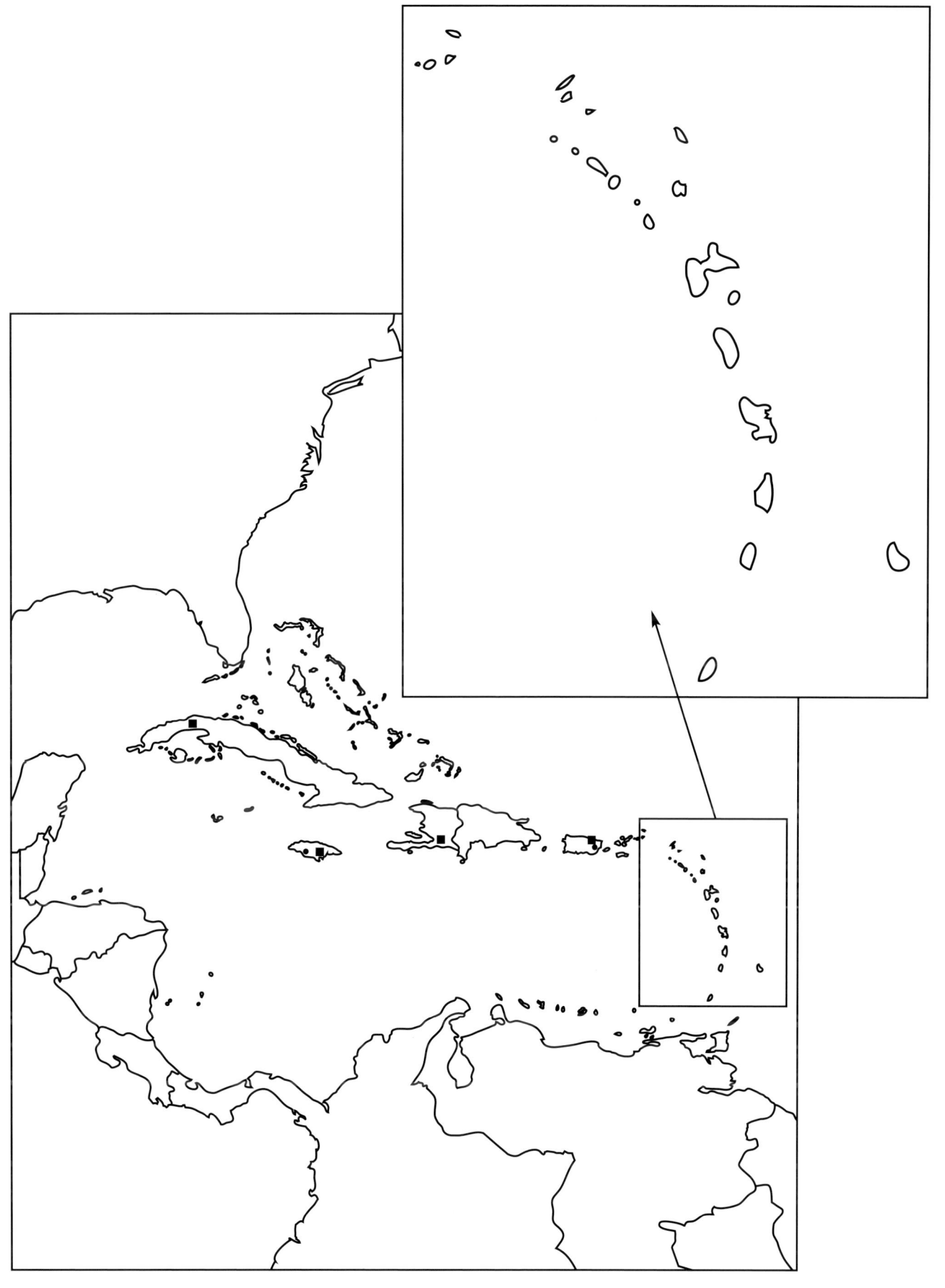

Índice

agricultura 15, 23
alimentos 20–21, 22, 23
amerindios 10
Antigua 5, 7, 24
Antillas Mayores 4, 5, 26
Antillas Menores 4, 5, 26

Bahamas 4, 5, 7, 14, 26
banderas 21, 26
Barbados 5, 7, 19, 25
Barbuda 5
Belice 4, 5

casas 18–19
ciudades 16–17, 18, 22, 23, 24, 27
clima 8–9, 25
Cuba 4, 5, 16, 18, 25, 26, 27

deportes 25
Dominica 5

empleos 12, 22–23
escuelas 12, 13, 22

familias 12, 13, 19
festivales 24

Granada 5, 9, 21
Guadalupe 5
Guyana 4, 5, 10

Haití 5, 12, 13, 17
huracanes 9

idiomas 10
Islas Vírgenes 5, 11

Jamaica 5, 11, 16, 19, 20

lluvia 8, 9

Mar Caribe 4, 5
Martinica 5, 15
monedas 27
montañas 6
música 24, 25, 29

niños 12, 13, 25

Océano Atlántico 4, 8

pesca 14, 23

plantaciones 12, 15, 23
playas 6, 7, 9, 14, 21, 25
Puerto Rico 5, 8, 20, 25

religiones 11
República Dominicana 5, 9, 12, 26, 27

San Cristóbal y Nevis 5
San Martín 5, 21, 22
San Vicente y las Granadinas 5
Santa Lucía 5, 6, 21, 23
Surinam 4, 5

Tobago 5
trabajo 15, 22–23
Trinidad 5, 13, 25
turistas 9, 22

vida urbana 14–15

Friends of the Houston Public Library

972.9 P   HACRX
Powell, Jillian.
Descubramos paGises del Caribe /

ACRES HOMES
05/10

E   J
796.332   c.1
FRI
Frisch
The history of the Minnesota Vikings

RL 6.8
Pts 0.5
2025

DISCARDED BY VERMILLION PUBLIC LIBRARY

Vermillion Public Library
18 Church Street
Vermillion, SD 57069
(605) 677-7060

DEMCO

THE HISTORY OF THE MINNESOTA VIKINGS

THE HISTORY OF THE MINNESOTA

Published by Creative Education
123 South Broad Street
Mankato, Minnesota 56001
Creative Education is an imprint of The Creative Company.

DESIGN AND PRODUCTION BY **EVANSDAY DESIGN**

Copyright © 2005 Creative Education.
International copyright reserved in all countries.
No part of this book may be reproduced in any form
without written permission from the publisher.
Printed in the United States of America

LIBRARY OF CONGRESS CATALOGING-IN-PUBLICATION DATA

Frisch, Aaron.
The history of the Minnesota Vikings / by Aaron Frisch.
p. cm. — (NFL today)
Summary: Traces the history of the team from its beginnings through 2003.
ISBN 1-58341-303-0
1. Minnesota Vikings (Football team)—History—Juvenile literature.
[1. Minnesota Vikings (Football team)—History. 2. Football—History.]
I. Title. II. Series.

GV956.M5F75 2004
796.332'64'09776579—dc22   2003062577

First edition

9 8 7 6 5 4 3 2 1

COVER PHOTO: quarterback Daunte Culpepper

VIKINGS

MINNESOTA IS A COLD PLACE. THE FALL SEASON IS SHORT, AND THEN SNOW AND ICE COVER THE STATE LIKE A BLANKET FOR UP TO SIX MONTHS UNTIL THE SPRING SUN FINALLY THAWS THE FROZEN LAND. BUT THE HARDY PEOPLE OF MINNESOTA DON'T HIBERNATE THROUGH THE CHILLY FALL AND LONG WINTER OF THE NORTH. THEY EMBRACE THE COLD, TAKING TO THE GREAT OUTDOORS TO HUNT, SKI, SKATE, RIDE SNOWMOBILES, AND ICE-FISH ON THE STATE'S COUNTLESS LAKES. SINCE 1961, MINNESOTANS HAVE ALSO GATHERED TO CHEER ON A TEAM IN THE NATIONAL FOOTBALL LEAGUE (NFL). THAT YEAR, A NEW FRANCHISE BUILT FROM SCRATCH SETTLED IN THE TWIN CITIES AREA OF MINNEAPOLIS AND ST. PAUL. THE CLUB WAS NAMED THE VIKINGS— TOUGH, PIRATE-LIKE SAILORS FROM ANOTHER NORTHERN REGION ACROSS THE OCEAN, SCANDINAVIA—AND WAS SOON RANSACKING THE NFL.

[Defensive end Carl Eller]

THE VIKINGS SET SAIL>

IT IS FITTING that the Vikings' history begins with a man named Winter—Max Winter. In the late 1950s, the Minnesota businessman began writing letters to the NFL commissioner seeking to establish a football franchise in Minnesota. In 1960, the league finally gave in to his repeated requests, and the Vikings were born.

Winter hired Norm Van Brocklin, a former NFL quarterback known for his short temper, as the team's first head coach. The original Vikings roster was made up mostly of unproven rookies and veterans cast off by other teams. Among the veterans was former star running back Hugh McElhenny, and the rookies included running back Tommy Mason, cornerback Ed Sharockman, and quarterback Fran Tarkenton.

No one expected much of the first-year Vikings, but they opened eyes around the league by crushing the

Iron-man end Jim Marshall made 127 quarterback sacks during his long and brilliant Vikings career.

Down! Black 7 Set! Hut!

Chicago Bears 37–13 in their first game. In the victory, Tarkenton proved that he was a rising star by passing for four touchdowns and running for another. The Vikings posted losing records their first few seasons, but Tarkenton's scrambling style—which often led pursuing defenders on wild chases through the backfield—never failed to thrill fans (and irritate his old-fashioned coach).

The defense was anchored in Minnesota's early years by Jim Marshall. One of the original Vikings, the 6-foot-4 and 240-pound end seemed indestructible; he spent 19 seasons with the Vikings and played in an NFL-record 282 consecutive games. Although his career featured countless highlights, many fans will always remember a famous "lowlight" that took place in 1964. In a game against the San Francisco 49ers that season, Marshall scooped up a fumble and raced into the end zone. Unfortunately, he had run the wrong direction, giving the 49ers two points for a safety.

With the addition of tough running back Bill Brown and kicker Fred Cox, the Vikings slowly improved, going 8–5–1 in 1964. Then problems developed on the sidelines. Coach Van Brocklin and Tarkenton often clashed, and the losses started piling up again. In 1967, Tarkenton was traded away, and Van Brocklin resigned.

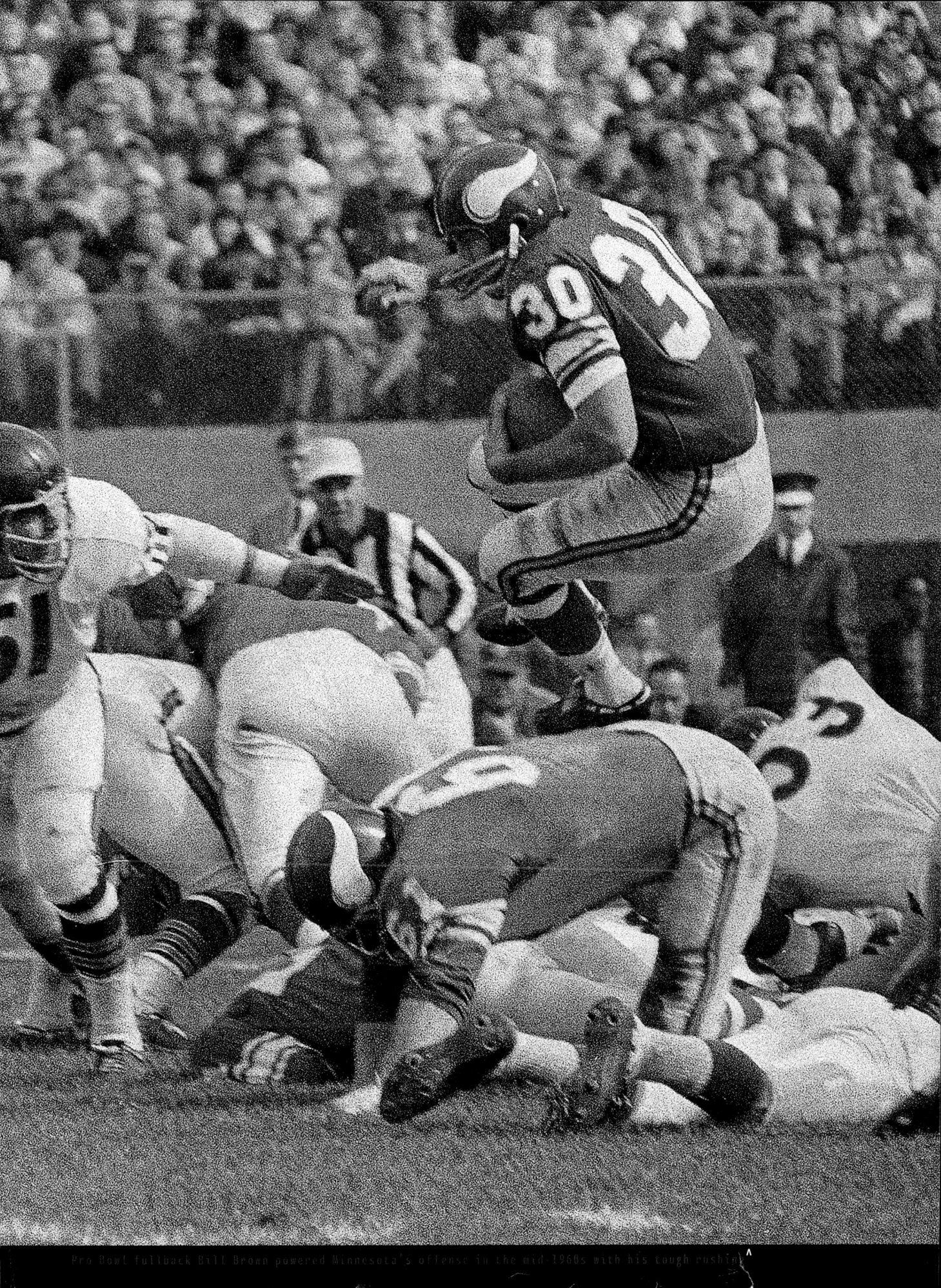

Pro Bowl fullback Bill Brown powered Minnesota's offense in the mid-1960s with his tough rushing.

THE GLORY YEARS>

MAX WINTER CHOSE Bud Grant as the team's next head coach. A former football and baseball standout at the University of Minnesota—and a former coach in the Canadian Football League—Grant was just the patient, determined leader the Vikings needed. A tall, stern figure with a steely gaze, he would remain the face of the Minnesota Vikings for 18 seasons.

In 1968, Grant and the Vikings won their first National Football Conference (NFC) Central Division title with an 8–6 record. Part of the credit went to scrappy quarterback Joe Kapp and safety Paul Krause. But the brightest stars were on the defensive line. Minnesota's line—made up of ends Jim Marshall and Carl Eller and tackles Alan Page and Gary Larsen—was among the NFL's best.

The fearsome "Purple People Eaters" made the Vikings a powerhouse in the late 1960s and most of the '70s.

Fran Tarkenton passed for an incredible 47,003 yards and 342 touchdowns during his NFL career

Charge 12 Charge 12! Set! Hut Hut!

All four players were amazingly quick and relentless in their pursuit. This fearsome front four, which became known as the "Purple People Eaters," followed a simple game plan: "Meet at the quarterback."

In 1969, the Vikings set sail for greatness. Kapp torched the Baltimore Colts with an NFL-record seven touchdown passes in the second game of the season. The Vikings won 11 more games in a row before beating the Cleveland Browns 27–7 in the championship game to win their first league title. As NFL champs, the Vikings then took on the Kansas City Chiefs of the rival American Football League (AFL) in the Super Bowl (in those days, the NFL champs played the AFL champs in the Super Bowl). The Vikings were heavily favored, but they could never get their offense going and lost 23–7.

Still, the good times were just starting in Minnesota. The Vikings ruled the NFC Central throughout the 1970s, winning the division eight times. In 1972, to the delight of many fans, Tarkenton returned and resumed scrambling across the frozen turf of Metropolitan Stadium. In 1975, Tarkenton—whom Grant called "the greatest quarterback ever in the NFL"—threw 25 touchdown passes and was named the NFL's Most Valuable Player (MVP).

With Tarkenton and running back Chuck Foreman leading a strong offense, and the Purple People Eaters continuing to devour opponents, the Vikings went 45–10–1 from 1973 to 1976 and returned to the Super Bowl three more times. Sadly, the biggest prize of all eluded them, as they lost each time. As the 1970s drew to a close, the Vikings were haunted by their Super Bowl losses: 23–7 to Kansas City in 1969; 24–7 to the Miami Dolphins in 1973; 16–6 to the Pittsburgh Steelers in 1974; and 32–14 to the Oakland Raiders in 1976.

A NEW BAND OF VIKINGS>

THE 1982 OPENING of the Hubert H. Humphrey Metrodome, an indoor stadium with a fiberglass roof, signaled the start of a new era for the Vikings. Old Metropolitan Stadium was torn down, and most of the team's former stars—including late-1970s receiver Ahmad Rashad—were replaced by a new band of Vikings.

Minnesota was a mediocre team for much of the 1980s. Quarterback Tommy Kramer ran the offense for many of those seasons, while the defense was led by linebacker Scott Studwell, tough safety Joey Browner, and defensive end Chris Doleman. All of these players played some great games under head coach Jerry Burns, who took over when Grant retired in 1985. Yet perhaps no Vikings player shone as brightly in the late '80s as receiver Anthony Carter.

Quarterback Tommy Kramer spent 13 seasons in Minnesota, setting many club passing records.

The performances of Anthony Carter helped propel the Vikings to some strong seasons in the late '80s

End 18! Set! Hut!

Carter joined Minnesota in 1985 after an amazing college career at the University of Michigan. Although he stood only 5-foot-11 and weighed just 175 pounds, Carter made up for his lack of size with terrific instincts and quickness. He also showed surprising speed, often streaking downfield to haul in long-range bombs. "I've always said that if the good Lord put anybody on this earth to play pro football, it was A.C.," said Coach Burns. "He just forgot to give him a body."

Carter's heroics and a tough defense helped the Vikings make the playoffs in 1987, 1988, and 1989. In the 1988 playoffs, the 8–7 Vikings stunned the sports world by beating the New Orleans Saints 44–10 and San Francisco 36–24 to reach the NFC championship game. The title game against the Washington Redskins was a close battle, but the Vikings fell just short of the Super Bowl, losing 17–10.

THE COACH GREEN ERA>

IN 1992, THE Vikings brought in former college coach Dennis Green as their new leader. At the time, the Vikings were best known for their defense. Luckily, Minnesota had just acquired a player Coach Green could build a mighty offense around, too: wide receiver Cris Carter.

Carter had been a great player in Philadelphia, but he had also struggled with drug and alcohol problems, and the Eagles cut him in 1991. The Vikings were more than willing to take a chance on the sure-handed receiver and claimed him for just a $100 waiver fee. In Minnesota, Carter turned his life around—freeing himself from substance abuse and becoming deeply religious—and put together a Hall of Fame career.

A sure Hall-of-Famer, Cris Carter was known for his great hands, strength, and clutch performances

Robert Smith was a college track star before becoming the Vikings' all-time leading rusher

John Randle led Minnesota in sacks from 1993 to 2000

Warren Moon was one of many 1990s Vikings passers

Carter's 6-foot-3 frame and terrific hands enabled him to catch virtually any pass, no matter how poorly thrown, and his confident and vocal personality made him essentially a coach on the field. In 1994, he set a new NFL record with 122 catches, many of them on high, "alley-oop" passes in which he outjumped defenders for the ball. "I always tell the quarterback, when in doubt, just throw it high and I'll go up and get it," Carter said.

Green and Carter led the Vikings back to power. Minnesota made the playoffs every year but one between 1992 and 2000, winning the NFC Central four times. A number of players contributed to these good times. Robert Smith, a tall running back with great speed, was drafted in 1993 and averaged more than 1,000 yards a season throughout the '90s. In 1994, veteran quarterback Warren Moon joined the Vikings and set a new team record by passing for 4,264 yards. And defensively, powerful and eccentric tackle John Randle was a nightmare for opposing quarterbacks.

Randall Cunningham threw 34 touchdown passes in 1998 as Minnesota rolled to its best record ever.

Yet making the playoffs was one thing; reaching the Super Bowl was another. The Vikings lost in the first round of the playoffs every year until 1997. Then, in one of the most thrilling games in franchise history, quarterback Randall Cunningham helped turn a 19–3 halftime deficit to the New York Giants into a stunning 23–22 victory. The Vikings were beaten a week later, but even better things were just around the corner.

PURPLE PRIDE>

IN 1998, THE Vikings franchise was bought by billionaire Red McCombs. The new owner introduced "Purple Pride" as the team's new battle cry, and he boldly predicted that Minnesota would go a perfect 16–0. Fortunately, the Vikings had just added a rookie receiver who would almost make that a reality: Randy Moss.

Moss had been a dominant college player. But he had also gotten into trouble with the law as a teenager, and 19 teams passed on him in the 1998 NFL Draft before Minnesota selected him. The Vikings knew they had lucked out. Moss stood 6-foot-4 and was a terrific leaper. Able to run the 40-yard dash in less than 4.3 seconds, he was also perhaps the fastest player in the NFL. "Moss is the scariest man in football and the best player, talentwise," Green Bay Packers coach Mike Sherman would later say. "You hold your breath every time they snap the ball."

Superstar Randy Moss averaged a stunning 1,395 receiving yards a year in his first six NFL seasons

Minnesota didn't go 16–0 as McCombs had predicted, but it came close. With a high-powered offense that included Cunningham, Carter, Moss, Smith, and a huge offensive line, the 1998 Vikings went 15–1 and set a new NFL record with 556 total points. Moss was especially spectacular, posting 1,313 receiving yards and scoring 17 touchdowns—both new league records for a rookie. In the playoffs, the Vikings crushed the Arizona Cardinals 41–21 to reach the NFC championship game.

Playing in front of a deafening Metrodome crowd, the Vikings roared out to a 20–7 lead over the Atlanta Falcons. But Minnesota's offense then sputtered, and the Falcons clawed back to tie the game at 27–27. In sudden-death overtime, Atlanta stopped the Vikings offense before kicking a game-winning field goal. The Vikings and their fans were devastated. "The Super Bowl is something you dream of as a kid," Moss said sadly, "and we had an opportunity to get there.... We let it slip right out of our hands."

Minnesota rebounded by making the playoffs again the next two seasons. In 2000, behind the great play of young quarterback Daunte Culpepper (who, at 6-foot-4 and 260 pounds, was the biggest quarterback of all time), Minnesota reached the NFC championship game again. But in one of the worst performances in team history, the Vikings

Despite his enormous size, Daunte Culpepper was one of the NFL's best scrambling quarterbacks

Like former star Robert Smith, Michael Bennett was a big-play rusher with frightening speed

were crushed 41–0 by the New York Giants. Soon after this embarrassing loss, a number of key leaders—including Coach Green, Carter, and Smith—left town or retired.

A new era dawned as Mike Tice, a former Vikings tight end, was named the team's head coach in 2002. Although the Vikings fell short of the playoffs in Tice's first two seasons, Minnesota fans remained confident. With an offense that featured Moss, Culpepper, and lightning-fast running back Michael Bennett—and with a defense anchored by tackle Kevin Williams and cornerback Antoine Winfield—the Vikings remained a dangerous team in the new NFC North Division.

The story of the Minnesota Vikings is one of success—and heartache. Although the team made the playoffs 23 times in its first 43 seasons, it has just one NFL championship to show for it, suffering painful losses in four Super Bowls and three conference championship games. As today's Vikings continue their voyage toward a Super Bowl trophy, they will continue to make those cold game days in the snowy North seem a little bit warmer.

INDEX >

B

Bennett, Michael 30–31, 31
Brown, Bill 8, 8–9
Browner, Joey 16
Burns, Jerry 16, 19

C

Carter, Anthony 16, 18–19, 19
Carter, Cris 20, 21, 23, 28, 31
Cox, Fred 8
Culpepper, Daunte 28, 28–29, 31
Cunningham, Randall 24–25, 25, 28

D

division championships 10, 13, 23
Doleman, Chris 16

E

Eller, Carl 5, 10, 13

F

Foreman, Chuck 14–15, 15

G

Grant, Bud 10, 13, 16
Green, Dennis 20, 23, 31

H

Hall of Fame 20
Hubert H. Humphrey Metrodome 16, 28

K

Kapp, Joe 10, 13
Kramer, Tommy 16, 17
Krause, Paul 10

L

Larsen, Gary 10, 13

M

Marshall, Jim 7, 8, 10, 13
Mason, Tommy 6
McCombs, Red 26, 28
McElhenny, Hugh 6
Metropolitan Stadium 13, 16
Moon, Warren 23, 23
Moss, Randy 26, 27, 28, 31

N

NFC championship games 19, 28, 31
NFL championship games 13
NFL championships 13, 31
NFL records 13, 23, 28

P

Page, Alan 10, 13
"Purple People Eaters" 11, 13, 15

R

Randle, John 23, 23
Rashad, Ahmad 16

S

Sharockman, Ed 6
Smith, Robert 22, 23, 28, 31
Studwell, Scott 16
Super Bowl 13, 15, 19, 28, 31

T

Tarkenton, Fran 6, 8, 12–13, 13, 15
team records 23
Tice, Mike 31

V

Van Brocklin, Norm 6, 8
Vikings name 4

W

Williams, Kevin 31
Winfield, Antoine 31
Winter, Max 6, 10